The Sa

The Sayings of

VIRGINIA
WOOLF

edited by
Luce Bonnerot

DUCKWORTH

First published in 1996 by
Gerald Duckworth & Co. Ltd.
The Old Piano Factory
48 Hoxton Square, London N1 6PB
Tel: 0171 729 5986
Fax: 0171 729 0015

A catalogue record for this book is available
from the British Library

ISBN 0 7156 2619 1

Typeset by Ray Davies
Printed in Great Britain by
Redwood Books Ltd., Trowbridge

Contents

To all my friends in England

Introduction

Although Virginia Woolf expressed herself on a wide range of subjects – often sensitive ones – with force and dignity, she never tried to preach or to impose her opinions on others. Her aim was to convince by developing arguments, using her imagination and experience; she was not fundamentally axiomatic. Also, though she was very witty, she did not flaunt her wit at every turn. In short, she was not a professional writer of 'bons mots' – but she could be ironical, sarcastic, provoking, with a kind of ferocity when judging people as she was able to see through their pretences and hollowness. She could also contradict herself – but then we know that only intelligent people change their minds.

All this means that the sayings included in this book have often been extracted from fairly long developments of her thoughts, arguments or meditations. Selecting them, cutting them from the mother branch so to speak, was not an easy task. Some particularly subtle sayings have had to be abandoned because they were so embedded in their context and subtext that it would have been necessary to quote whole pages for their real meaning to emerge. The selection of topics naturally follows the subjects of her thinking and writing, and these sayings are taken from her novels, letters, essays and criticism.

This said, the sayings do not come in great numbers from her novels, for these are essentially poetic and lyrical explorations of human inwardness, probings into the mystery and silence of the human soul, with intense attention given to generally unheard echoes and unfelt rhythms of life. Furthermore, as we all know, an extract taken from what a character says in a novel does not necessarily and automatically represent the novelist's opinion. Without going into the much debated question of Virginia Woolf 's ability or inability to create characters, I have been prepared to take some risks when I have recognized the authorial voice, not only in the narrator but also in the characters. Virginia Woolf 's work is a chamber of echoes: the more one reads her, the more one hears them. Therefore I have felt entitled to take up some of the characters' pronouncements, say in *Jacob's Room* or *The Waves* (where there are no real characters but one voice speaking through different names and sexes), and put them down as Virginia Woolf 's sayings. A further difficulty with the novels is that they are a poetic rendering of the psychological complexity and elusiveness of individual personalities and, in consequence, do not offer easy generalizations about human behaviour or the affairs of men.

In Virginia Woolf 's non-fiction, two books stand out in their expression of her thinking about women: *A Room of One's Own* (1929) and *Three Guineas* (1938) – the latter having to be read in conjunction with the novel *The Years* (1937). *Three Guineas* is a violent denunciation of the educational deprivation that 'the daughters of educated men' had had to endure for so long. The book is an equally violent and brave protest against war, for which she felt that the male instinct for fighting and love of military glory – as well as unchecked male power all over the world – were responsible.

Born in 1882, Virginia Woolf knew by experience

what Victorian womanhood endured: complete
suppression outside the spheres of the home,
marriage and maternity, with only one role to play
– that of the Angel in the House. Forty years or so
passed before she dared express directly and
publicly her revolt against the subjection of women
to male power (the hated 'patriarchy') and openly
reveal her own brand of feminism, within which
she did not consider herself a feminist. What she
clamoured for was freedom and equality for
women, not a victory of one sex over the other; she
believed in and for once got very near to preaching
a sharing of the qualities and characteristics of each
sex so that each individual could become a
complete human being. *Orlando* is a witty and
brilliant plea for the effacement of differences: man
or woman, Orlando is the same person and only the
clothes he/she has to wear and the part he/she is
expected to play in society are different. The
sudden change from man to woman for Orlando
was naturally the ideal opportunity for Virginia
Woolf to expose the absurdity of conventions
regulating the relations between the sexes and to
write the most delightfully comic scenes about
them. Witness Orlando the woman discovering that
the sight of her ankles and a little bit of calf so
inflamed a sailor perched on a mast (on board the
ship that was bringing her back to England) that he
almost fell to his death. With feigned contrition,
Orlando concluded that 'in all humanity', she had
to keep her ankles covered. And her further
meditation on the subject is expressed in terms that
have overtones of a burning actuality (when we
consider the condition of many women in the
world).

   Some sayings appear under the heading: 'Other
writers', and the reader is entitled to a brief

consideration of Virginia Woolf 's critical activity. She was both a critic and a reviewer – the reviewing being done essentially to earn money. Books in general attracted her human sympathy, but her judgment on the finished literary product could be far from sympathetic. She may have called two books of her essays *The Common Reader*, but common reader she was not. Her criticism was a creator's criticism – which probably explains the height from which she was able to consider a work and the assurance with which she distributed blame and praise, following her own subtle understanding and aesthetic convictions rather than external critical theories. Constraints of space have precluded the inclusion of all or even part of her pronouncements on the work of the great names of the past. I have decided to give none and concentrate instead on her reactions to the work of three of her contemporaries who were indeed rivals: James Joyce, D.H. Lawrence and Katherine Mansfield. The results are astonishing, considering Virginia Woolf 's intelligence and culture. She erected a barrier of incomprehension between Joyce, Lawrence and herself, denigrating their work without – she had to admit – reading them seriously.Katherine Mansfield she treated a little better, especially after the writer's death. Were the three of them such a threat to her supremacy in what she considered her reserved territory, that of shaping the 'new novel'? Her famous phrase: 'No creative writer can swallow a contemporary' seems a defensive generalization behind which she could hide a more personal reaction of jealousy and alarm. Reading her carefully, one can feel there existed in her a genuine fear for her own creativity, probably the well-known 'anxiety of influence'.

Only a very short selection of Virginia Woolf 's

recorded thoughts about her art as a writer is given in this book, mainly from *A Writer's Diary*. I can only hope that these twenty or so sayings will give a true idea of the passionate dialogue she conducted with herself over the years about what she was trying to achieve in her writing (and at what cost). It was this passion for literature, for writing, which made her live, for as long as she could. Testimony to this are her searching questions about the nature of art and what she was trying to express in her novels, her continual meditation on the mystery of the creative power in which she both lost and saved herself, and her anguished questioning of the ultimate value of her work and her reputation as an artist.

In the same section, entitled 'On Herself ', a few autobiographical sayings are offered as a reminder of Virginia Woolf 's character: her rebelliousness, her independence of mind and dignity, her courage, the emotional tensions within her, and her tragic view of life. This last increased in 1940 with the Nazi threat, which she saw as the possible end of civilization, heralding a reign of barbarism which would engulf everyone, and particularly her Jewish husband and herself. How moving to read in her diary, dated 22 June 1940: 'I can't conceive that there will be a 27 June 1941' – knowing as we do that on 28 March 1941, she would drown herself in the river Ouse. The fear of a German invasion was not the only factor which drove her to commit suicide. She believed that her power as an artist was deserting her – the creative power that had sustained her and helped her to fight despair by putting into words the subtle insights she brought back from her perilous forays into the human psyche. One must remember, however, that the sombre side of her nature existed concurrently with a sunny one, with a fervent love of life and friends. She was as sensitive to the sweetness and sensuousness of life as she was to its fierceness and cruelty. In fact her capacity for joy was immense and her writing shows us her extraordinary sensibility to every single sensation, among them those that came from the world of nature as her body registered and stored with gratitude all that was offered: the warmth of the sun, the freshness and fluidity of the waves, the greenness of tree and meadow. Her enjoyment of the good things in life, among them wine and fine food (except in dreadful moments of illness) could be no less keen. One of her pronouncements on the pleasure of eating roast duck is positively Keatsian!

Needless to say, the preparation of this selection of her sayings has been made possible by the admirable work of those who produced the editions of her *Letters* and *Diaries*. There were other sources but these two were among the most important. In the last quotation of this book, she speaks of 'a monstrous growth' of biography and criticism when – she says – reading a writer's work should be sufficient to discover all that we want to know. True, there is such a thing as a literary industry. But in the case of Virginia Woolf, the industry strikes one as of exceptional quality and testifies to the fascination that her personality and work continue to exert.

A collection of sayings like this is bound to be an appetizer for those who have not hitherto read much of Virginia Woolf 's work: surely they will want to discover more; for those who read her some time ago, no doubt this will be a poignant reminder of phrases they had loved and half forgotten. Among her admirers and devotees, a great number will probably look for their favourite phrases and be disappointed if they cannot find them all. But any anthology or collection of literary items implies a choice, and every choice is subjective.

I am only too conscious, on bringing this introduction to a close, of the myriad thoughts left outside, of the unsaid beneath and around the said. Virginia Woolf 's 'écriture' is one of such resonances, of such transparency and multiplicity that one might well despair of ever deciphering all the signs she has left us. But her sayings live in us and may, in time, blossom.

Sources

Dates of publication are important for a full appreciation of the sayings, and they are given in the following list. The first two books were published by Duckworth and all the others by the Hogarth Press.

The Voyage Out, 1915
Night and Day, 1919
Monday or Tuesday, 1921
Jacob's Room, 1922
Mr Bennett and Mrs Brown, 1924
The Common Reader, 1925
Mrs Dalloway, 1925
To the Lighthouse, 1927
Orlando: A Biography, 1928
A Room of One's Own, 1929
The Waves, 1931
A Letter to a Young Poet, 1932
The Common Reader, Second Series, 1932
Flush: A Biography, 1933
Walter Sickert: A Conversation, 1934
The Years, 1937

Three Guineas, 1938
Roger Fry: A Biography, 1940
Between the Acts, 1941
The Death of the Moth and Other Essays, 1942
The Moment and Other Essays, 1947
The Captain's Death Bed and Other Essays, 1950

A Writer's Diary, ed. Leonard Woolf, 1953
The Letters of Virginia Woolf, 6 vols, ed. Nigel Nicolson & Joanne Trautmann, 1975-1980
Virginia Woolf: Moments of Being, ed. Jeanne Schulkind, 1976
The Diary of Virginia Woolf, ed. Anne Olivier Bell & Andrew MacNeillie, 5 vols, 1977-1984

On Herself

And more and more I come to loathe any dominion
of one over another; any leadership, any imposition
of the will.   *A Writer's Diary*, 19 March 1919

Only the thought of people suffering more than I
do at all consoles; and that is an aberration of
egotism, I suppose.
                                               A Writer's Diary, 18 August 1921

What a born melancholic I am! The only way I keep
afloat is by working …. Directly I stop working I
feel that I am sinking down, down.
                                               A Writer's Diary, 23 June 1929

Take away my love for my friends and my burning
and pressing sense of the importance and lovability
and curiosity of human life and I should be nothing
but a membrane, a fibre, uncoloured, lifeless to be
thrown away like any other excreta.
                                               Letter, 19 August 1930

The Prime Minister's letter offering to recommend
me for the Companion of Honour. No.
                                               A Writer's Diary, 13 May 1935

… questions about my concern with the art of
writing. On the whole the art becomes absorbing –
more? no, I think it's been absorbing ever since I
was a little creature, scribbling a story in the
manner of Hawthorne on the green plush sofa in
the drawing room at St Ives ….
                                               A Writer's Diary, 19 December 1938

Churchill exhorting all men to stand together ....
But though L. says he has petrol in the garage for
suicide should Hitler win, we go on.

A Writer's Diary, 13 May 1940

The great battle which decides our life or death
goes on.

A Writer's Diary, 7 June 1940

The pressure of this battle wipes out London pretty
quick. A gritting day. A sample of my present
mood I reflect: capitulation will mean All Jews to be
given up. Concentration camps. So to our garage.

A Writer's Diary, 9 June 1940

Further, the war – our waiting while the knives
sharpen for the operation – has taken away the
outer wall of security. ... We pour to the edge of a
precipice ... and then? I can't conceive that there
will be a 27th June 1941.

A Writer's Diary, 22 June 1940

But I do feel myself that I ought to have been able
to make not merely thousands of people interested
in literature; but millions.

A Writer's Diary, 24 August 1940

I am so old I could write a life of myself. But I
remember too much.

Letter, 8 September 1940

Is the time coming when I can endure to read my
own writing in print without blushing – shivering
and wishing to take cover?

A Writer's Diary, 27 March 1919

What sort of diary should I like mine to be?
Something loose knit and yet not slovenly, so
elastic that it will embrace any thing, solemn, slight
or beautiful that comes into my mind. I should like
it to resemble some deep old desk, or capacious
hold-all, in which one flings a mass of odds and
ends without looking them through.

A Writer's Diary, 20 April 1919

There's no doubt in my mind that I have found out
how to begin (at 40) to say something in my own
voice; and that interests me so that I feel I can go
ahead without praise.   *A Writer's Diary*, 26 July 1922

When I write I am merely a sensibility.

A Writer's Diary, 22 August 1922

Have I the power of conveying the true reality? Or
do I write essays about myself?

A Writer's Diary, 19 June 1923

I have an idea that I will invent a new name for my
books to supplant 'novel'. A new —— by Virginia
Woolf. But what? Elegy?

A Writer's Diary, 27 June 1925

Thought of my own power of writing with
veneration, as of something incredible belonging to
someone else; never again to be enjoyed by me.

A Writer's Diary, Rodmell 1926

The insatiable desire to write something before I
die, this ravaging sense of the shortness and
feverishness of life, make me cling, like a man on a
rock, to my one anchor.

A Writer's Diary, 20 December 1927

... What I want now to do is to saturate every atom.
I mean to eliminate all waste, deadness, superfluity:
to give the moment whole; whatever it includes.
Say that the moment is a combination of thought;
sensation, the voice of the sea. ... Why admit
anything to literature that is not poetry – by which I
mean saturated?

A Writer's Diary, 28 November 1928

... And then they say I write beautifully! How
could I write beautifully when I am always trying
to say something that has not been said, and should
be said for the first time, exactly.

Letter, 15-17 March 1930

All writing is nothing but putting words on the
backs of rhythm.   Letter, 7 April 1930

A very good summer, this, for all my shying &
jibbing, my tremors this morning. Beautifully quiet,
airy, powerful. I believe I want this more humane
existence for my next – to spread carelessly among
one's friends – to feel the width & amusement of
human life: not to strain to make a pattern just yet:
to be made supple, & to let the juice of usual things,
talk, character, seep through me, quietly,
involuntarily before I say – Stop, & take out my pen.

A Writer's Diary, 20 August 1932

Odd how the creative power at once brings the
whole universe to order.

A Writer's Diary, 27 July 1934

Why do I always fight shy of my contemporaries?
What is really the woman's angle? ... Do I
instinctively keep my mind from analysing which
would impair its creativeness? ... No creative
writer can swallow another contemporary.

A Writer's Diary, 20 April 1935

And so I go on to suppose that the shock-receiving
capacity is what makes me a writer. I hazard the
explanation that a shock is at once in my case
followed by the desire to explain it. I feel that I have
had a blow; but it is not, as I thought as a child,
simply a blow from an enemy hidden behind the
cotton wool of daily life; it is or will become a
revelation of some order; it is a token of some real
thing behind appearances; and I make it real by
putting it into words.

Moments of Being: A Sketch of the Past

What I had feared was that I was dismissed as
negligible.

A Writer's Diary, 12 April 1921

The only review I am anxious about is the one in
the *Supt.*: not that it will be the most intelligent, but
it will be the most read and I can't bear to see me
clowned in public.

A Writer's Diary, 14 October 1922

Now suppose I might become one of the interesting
– I will not say great – but interesting novelists?
Oddly, for all my vanity, I have not until now had
much faith in my novels, or thought them my own
expression.

A Writer's Diary, 20 April 1925

I will not be 'famous', 'great'. I will go on adventuring, changing, opening my mind and my eyes, refusing to be stamped and stereotyped.

A Writer's Diary, 29 October 1933

Well: do I think I shall be among the English novelists after my death?

A Writer's Diary, 11 October 1934

English Society

We dont belong to any 'class'; we thinkers: might as well be French or German. Yet I am English in some way –.

Diary, 22 September 1928

... of course our carriage was quite full – golf playing stockbrokers who began by saying that it was the poor who did all the eating and over eating and then fell asleep – disgusting hogs.

Letter, 30 October 1917

I had to go to the dentist in Wigmore St. on Monday, at 3, and by 4 the streets were in such a state that if I hadn't met L. ... everyone seemed half drunk – beer bottles were passed round – every wounded soldier was kissed, by women; nobody had any notion where to go or what to do; it poured steadily; crowds drifted up and down the pavements waving flags and jumping into omnibuses, but in such a disorganised, half hearted, sordid state that I felt more and more melancholy and hopeless of the human race.

The London poor, half drunk and very sentimental or completely stolid with their hideous voices and clothes and bad teeth, make one doubt whether it matters if we're at war or peace. But I suppose the poor wretches haven't much notion how to express their feelings.

Letter, 13 November 1918

... English society being what it is, no very great
merit is required, once you bear a well-known
name, to put you into a position where it is easier
on the whole to be eminent than obscure.

Night and Day, III

They die very beautifully, the aristocracy; there's
that to be said for them. But I stirred my breast for
any cinder of romance – I stirred among the
cinders, it should be; and found nothing but
benevolence and boredom.

I made this profound observation that the
aristocracy is hopelessly amateurish. In youth this
has a certain charm; in age it is a little banal.

Letter, 13 May 1921

They [the young] talk love where we talked God. I
think our age though ossified was of the two the
more sublime.

Letter, 1 November 1928

Looked at from the gypsy point of view, a Duke,
Orlando understood, was nothing but a profiteer or
robber who snatched land and money from people
who rated these things of little worth, and could
think of nothing better to do than to build three
hundred and sixty-five bed-rooms when one was
enough and none was even better than one. She
could not deny that her ancestors had accumulated
field after field; house after house; honour after
honour, yet had none of them been saints or heroes,
or great benefactors of the human race.

Orlando, III

What depresses me is that the workers seem to have taken on all the middle class respectabilities which we – at any rate if we are any good at writing or painting – have faced and thrown out.

Letter, 10 October 1930

The flower show was a mass of cold mud and blazing blossom and petrified faces. Oh the country gentlemen of England and their riddled, raddled foxhunting wives!

Letter, 25 May 1932

How I hated marrying a Jew – how I hated their nasal voices, and their oriental jewellery, and their noses and their wattles – What a snob I was: for they have immense vitality, and I think I like that quality best of all. They cant die – they exist on a handful of rice and a thimble of water – their flesh dries on their bones, but still they pullulate, copulate and amass ... millions of money.

Letter, 2 August 1930

One is supposed to pass over class distinctions in silence; one person is supposed to be as well born as another; and yet English fiction is so steeped in the ups and downs of social rank that without them it would be unrecognisable.

It is useless to suppose that social distinctions have vanished. Each may pretend that he knows no such restrictions, and that the compartment in which he lives allows him the run of the world. But it is an illusion.

It seems, therefore, that the novelist, and the English novelist in particular, suffers from a disability which affects no other artist to the same extent. His work is influenced by his birth. He is fated to know intimately, and so to describe with understanding, only those who are of his own social rank. He cannot escape from the box in which he has been bred.

It is from the middle class that writers spring, because it is in the middle class only that the practice of writing is as natural and habitual as hoeing a field or building a house.

The Common Reader, Second Series: The Niece of an Earl

But they're not interested in other people's children, he observed. Only in their own; their own property; their own flesh and blood, which they would protect with the unsheathed claws of the primeval swamp ....

The Years: Present Day

I suppose you are one of the people – they are almost unknown in England – who can make a lecture exciting. Is it your Latin blood? I would rather sit in a cellar or watch spiders than listen to an Englishman lecturing.

Letter, 2 September 1937

Our young writers have a sentimental and emotional love for 'the poor'. They know nothing and care nothing – that is snobbishness partly – about the great. Now that Lady Ottoline is dead, perhaps there are no salons where the classes meet.

Letter, 5 October 1938

Art is the first luxury to be discarded in times of stress; the artist is the first of the workers to suffer. But intellectually also he depends upon society. Society is not only his paymaster but his patron.

The Moment: The Artist and Politics

The snob is a flutter-brained, hare-brained creature so little satisfied with his or her own standing that in order to consolidate it he or she is always flourishing a title or an honour in other people's faces so that they may believe and help him to believe what he does not really believe – that he or she is somehow a person of importance.

Moments of Being: Am I a Snob?

Royalty to begin with, merely as an experiment in the breeding of human nature, is of great psychological interest. For centuries a certain family has been segregated; bred with a care only lavished upon race-horses; splendidly housed, clothed and fed; abnormally stimulated in some ways, suppressed in others; worshipped, stared at, and kept shut up, as lions and tigers are kept, in a beautiful brightly lit room behind bars. The psychological effect upon them must be profound; and the effect upon us is as remarkable. Sane men and women as we are, we cannot rid ourselves of the superstition that there is something miraculous about these people shut up in their cage.

The Moment: Royalty

Politics

I think politicians and journalists must be the lowest of God's creatures, creeping perpetually in the mud, and biting with one end and stinging with the other ....
Letter, May 1908

Do you ever take that side of politics into account – the inhuman side, and how all the best feelings are shrivelled? It is the same with philanthropy, and that is why it attracts the bloodless women who dont care for their own relations.
Letter, December 1910

... I have now declared myself a Fabian.
Diary, 23 January 1915

... the Lords have passed the Suffrage Bill. I don't feel much more important – perhaps slightly so.
Diary, 11 January 1918

My aunt, Mary Beton, I must tell you, died by a fall from her horse .... The news of my legacy reached me one night about the same time that the act was passed that gave votes to women. A solicitor's letter fell into the post-box and ... I found that she had left me five hundred pounds a year for ever. Of the two – the vote and the money – the money, I own, seemed infinitely the more important.
A Room of One's Own, II

That's what I always want – instant and violent changes.
Letter, 6 June 1929

And here I am plagued by the sudden wish to write an Anti fascist Pamphlet. L. & I ... had a long discussion about all the things I might put in my pamphlet.

Diary, 26 February 1935

Justice! Liberty! ... What do they mean by Justice and Liberty? he asked, all these nice young men with two or three hundred a year. Something's wrong, he thought; there's a gap, a dislocation, between the word and the reality. If they want to reform the world ... why not begin there, at the centre, with themselves?

The Years: Present Day

Last night we had a meeting, to discuss politics here. The villagers all sat silent. The middle classes talked.

Letter, 5 October 1938

... another picture has imposed itself .... It is the figure of a man; some say, others deny, that he is Man himself, the quintessence of virility, the perfect type of which all the others are imperfect adumbrations. He is a man certainly. His eyes are glazed; his eyes glare. His body, which is braced in an unnatural position, is tightly cased in a uniform. Upon the breast of that uniform are sewn several medals and other mystic symbols. His hand is upon a sword. He is called in German and Italian Führer or Duce. And behind him lie ruined houses and dead bodies – men, women and children.

... The public and private worlds are inseparably connected; ... the tyrannies and servilities of the one are the tyrannies and servilities of the other.

But the human figure even in a photograph

suggests other and more complex emotions. It suggests that we cannot dissociate ourselves from that figure but are ourselves that figure. It suggests that we are not passive spectators doomed to unresisting obedience but by our thoughts and actions can ourselves change that figure.

Three Guineas, III

Hitlers are bred by slaves.

The Death of the Moth: Thoughts on Peace in an Air Raid

My puzzle is, ought artists now to become politicians? my instinct says no; but I'm not sure that I can justify my instinct.

Letter, 24 August 1940

England & Patriotism

And then, the passion of my life, that is the City of
London – to see London all blasted, that too raked
my heart. Have you that feeling for certain alleys
and little courts, between Chancery Lane and the
City? I walked to the Tower the other day by way
of caressing my love of all that.

Letter, 11 September 1940

London looked merry and hopeful, wearing her
wounds like stars; why do I dramatise London
perpetually? When I see a great smash like a
crushed match box where an old house stood I
wave my hand to London.

Letter, 25 September 1940

It's odd how England suddenly takes shape – not
that I have any patriotic pride – only a visual lust,
and a sense of Shakespeare.

Letter, 26 December 1936

Therefore if you [an educated man] insist upon
fighting to protect me, or 'our' country, let it be
understood, soberly and rationally between us, that
you are fighting to gratify a sex instinct which I
cannot share; to procure benefits which I have not
shared and probably will not share; but not to
gratify my instincts, or to protect either myself or
my country. 'For,' the outsider will say, 'in fact, as a
woman, I have no country. As a woman I want no
country. As a woman my country is the whole
world.' And if, when reason has said its say, still
some obstinate emotion remains, some love of

England dropped into a child's ears by the cawing of rooks in an elm tree, by the splash of waves on a beach, or by English voices murmuring nursery rhymes, this drop of pure, if irrational, emotion she will make serve her to give to England first what she desires of peace and freedom for the whole world.

Three Guineas, III

... of course I am 'patriotic': that is English, the language, farms, dogs, people: only we must enlarge the imaginative, and take stock of the emotion.

Letter, 7 June 1938

As for patriotism, I expect I have it as strong in me as you .... If we emphasise our position as outsiders and come to think it a natural distinction it should be easier for us than for those unfortunate young men who are shot through the sausage machine of Eton – King's or Christ Church.

Letter, 10 June 1938

Odd how often I think with what is love I suppose of the City: of the walk to the Tower: that is my England; I mean, if a bomb destroyed one of those little alleys with the brass bound curtains & the river smell & the old woman reading I should feel – well, what the patriots feel ....

Diary, 2 February 1940

Then I shall walk, all along the Thames, in and out where I used to haunt, so through the Temple, up the Strand and out into Oxford Street .... You never shared my passion for that great city. Yet it's what, in some odd corner of my dreaming mind, represents Chaucer, Shakespeare, Dickens. It's my only patriotism: save one vision, in Warwickshire one spring (May 1934) when we were driving back from Ireland and I saw a stallion being led, under the may and the beeches, along a grass ride; and I thought that is England.

Letter, 12 January 1941

Religion & the Church

Nothing comes up to the Church Service in these old Cathedrals; though I don't believe a word of it and never shall. Still the language and the sentiment of it all are dignified and grand above words.

Letter, 30 October 1904

The self-conceit of Christians is really unendurable.

Letter, Christmas Day 1910

That I believe is still the chief enemy – the fear of God.

Diary, 9 July 1918

… she [Clarissa] thought there were no Gods; no one was to blame; and so she evolved this atheist's religion of doing good for the sake of goodness.

Mrs Dalloway

Nothing, however, can be more arrogant, though nothing is commoner than to assume that of Gods there is only one, and of religions none but the speaker's.

Orlando, IV

But what pious thoughts it roused in Orlando, what evil passions it soothed asleep, who dare say, seeing that of all communions this with the deity is the most inscrutable? Novelist, poet, historian all falter with their hand on that door; nor does the believer himself enlighten us, for is he more ready to die than other people, or more eager to share his goods?

Orlando, IV

Irreligious as I am (to your eyes) I have a devout belief in the human soul – when I meet what can be called such emphatically.

Letter, 3 September 1930

We cannot make laws and religions that fit because we do not know ourselves.

The Years, 1917

He wasn't such a bad fellow, the Rev. G.W. Streatfield; a piece of traditional church furniture; a corner cupboard; or the top beam of a gate, fashioned by generations of village carpenters after some lost-in-the-mists-of-antiquity model.

Between the Acts

… There's Mr. Streatfield, going, I suppose to take the evening service. He'll have to hurry, or he won't have time to change …. He said she [Miss La Trobe] meant we all act. Yes, but whose play?

Between the Acts

Death

Nor were the deaths of young people really the
saddest things in life – they were saved so much;
they kept so much.

The Voyage Out, XXVI

Death was defiance. Death was an attempt to
communicate, people feeling the impossibility of
reaching the centre which, mystically, evaded them;
closeness drew apart; rapture faded; one was alone.
There was an embrace in death.

Mrs Dalloway

I found myself thinking with intense curiosity
about death. Yet if I'm persuaded of anything, it is
of mortality – Then why this sense that death is
going to be a great excitement? something positive;
active?

Letter, 19 November 1926

Life is as I've said since I was 10, awfully
interesting – if anything, quicker, keener at 44 than
24 – more desperate I suppose, as the river shoots
to Niagara – my new vision of death; active,
positive, like all the rest, exciting; & of great
importance – as an experience.

The one experience I shall never describe ....

Diary, 23 November 1926

But this brush with death was instructive & odd.
Had I woken in the divine presence it wd have
been with fists clenched & fury on my lips. 'I don't
want to come here at all!' So I should have
exclaimed. I wonder if this is the general state of
people who die violently. If so figure the condition
of Heaven after a battle.

Diary, 2 September 1930

What enemy do we now perceive advancing
against us, you whom I ride now, as we stand
pawing this stretch of pavement? It is death. Death
is the enemy ...
... Against you I will fling myself, unvanquished
and unyielding, O Death!

The Waves: 'Now to sum up'

... I thought, as I was dressing, how interesting it
would be to describe the approach of age, and the
gradual coming of death. As people describe love.

A Writer's Diary, 7 August 1939

Oh I try to imagine how one's killed by a bomb.
I've got it fairly vivid – the sensation: but cant see
anything but suffocating nonentity following after.
I shall think – oh I wanted another 10 years – not
this – & shant, for once, be able to describe it. It – I
mean death; no, the scrunching & scrambling, the
crushing of my bone shade in on my very active
eye & brain: the process of putting out the light, –
painful? Yes. Terrifying. I suppose so – Then a
swoon; a drum; two or three gulps attempting
consciousness & then, dot dot dot.

A Writer's Diary, 2 October 1940

Love, Sex & Marriage

What I meant was that *sexual* relations bore me more than they used. Am I a prude? Am I feminine? ... love is a disease; a frenzy; an epidemic; oh but how dull, how monotonous, and reducing its young men and women to what abysses of mediocrity!

Letter, 3 October 1924

... our mean lives, unsightly as they are, put on splendour and have meaning only under the eyes of love.

The Waves: 'I have signed my name', said Louis

... they are aware of each other; they live in each other; what else is love ...

The Years: Present Day

In every human being a vacillation from one sex to the other takes place, and often it is only the clothes that keep the male or female likeness, while underneath the sex is the very opposite of what it is above.

Orlando, IV

At any rate, when a subject is highly controversial – and any question about sex is that – one cannot hope to tell the truth.

A Room of One's Own, I

The society of buggers has many advantages – if you are a woman. It is simple, it is honest, it makes one feel, as I noted, in some respects at one's ease.

Moments of Being: Old Bloomsbury

One has a profound, if irrational, instinct in favour of the theory that the union of man and woman makes for the greatest satisfaction, the most complete happiness.

A Room of One's Own, VI

… to be engaged to marry some one with whom you are not in love is an inevitable step in a world where the existence of passion is only a traveller's story brought from the heart of deep forests and told so rarely that wise people doubt whether the story can be true.

Night and Day, XVII

When two people have been married for years they seem to become unconscious of each other's bodily presence so that they move as if alone, speak aloud things they do not expect to be answered and in general seem to experience all the comfort of solitude without its loneliness.

The Voyage Out, XV

As for thinking that I should have exhorted you to go to a marriage service, I can only say last time I went to one I had much ado not to stand up and cry out on the disgusting nature of it.

Letter, 27 March 1937

Women & Men

It's the beginning of the twentieth century and until a few years ago no woman had ever come out by herself and said things at all. There it was, going in the background, for all those thousands of years, this curious silent unrepresented life.

The Voyage Out, XVI

'I believe we [men] must have the sort of power over you that we're said to have over horses. They see us three times as big as we are or they'd never obey us. For that very reason, I'm inclined to doubt you'll ever do anything even when you have the vote.'

The Voyage Out, XVI

Who shall deny that this blankness of mind when combined with profusion, mother wit, old wives' tales, haphazard ways, moments of astonishing daring, humour, and sentimentality – who shall deny that in these respects every woman is nicer than any man?

Jacob's Room, I

As for the beauty of women, it is like the light on the sea, never constant to a single wave. They all have it; they all lose it.

Jacob's Room, X

If one could be friendly with women, what a pleasure – the relationship so secret & private compared with relations with men.

A Writer's Diary, 1 November 1924

... she could not resist sometimes yielding to the charm of a woman, not a girl, of a woman confessing, as to her they often did, some scrape, some folly. And whether it was pity, or their beauty, or that she was older, or some accident – like a faint scent, or a violin next door (so strange is the power of sounds at certain moments), she did undoubtedly then feel what men felt.

Mrs Dalloway

Love, the poet has said, is women's whole existence. And if we look for a moment at Orlando writing at her table .... Surely, since she is a woman and a beautiful woman, and a woman in the prime of life, she will soon give over this pretence of writing and thinking and begin at least to think of a gamekeeper (and as long as she thinks of a man, nobody objects to a woman thinking). And then she will write him a little note (and as long as she writes little notes nobody objects to a woman writing either) ....

Orlando, VI

Do not blush. Let us admit in the privacy of our own society that these things sometimes happen. Sometimes women do like women.

A Room of One's Own, V

... the daughters of educated men have always done their thinking from hand to mouth; not under green lamps at study tables in the cloisters of secluded colleges.

Three Guineas, II

The very word 'society' sets tolling in memory the dismal bells of a harsh music: shall not, shall not, shall not. You shall not learn; you shall not earn; you shall not own.

Three Guineas, III

What is a woman? I assure you, I do not know. I do
not believe that you know. I do not believe that
anybody can know until she has expressed herself
in all the arts and professions open to human skill.
The Death of the Moth: Professions for Women

The cheapness of writing paper is, of course, the
reason why women have succeeded as writers
before they have succeeded in the other professions.
The Death of the Moth: Professions for Women

… a woman must have money and a room of her
own if she is to write fiction ….
A Room of One's Own, I

… it would have been impossible, completely and
entirely, for any woman to have written the plays
of Shakespeare in the age of Shakespeare.
A Room of One's Own, III

I discovered that if I were going to review books I
should need to do battle with a certain phantom.
And the phantom was a woman, and when I came
to know her better I called her after the heroine of a
famous poem, The Angel in the House …. It was
she who bothered me and wasted my time and so
tormented me that at last I killed her ….

… you may not know what I mean by the Angel
in the House. I will describe her as shortly as I can.
She was intensely sympathetic. She was immensely
charming. She was utterly unselfish. She excelled in
the difficult arts of family life. She sacrificed herself

daily. If there was chicken, she took the leg; if there was a draught she sat in it – in short she was so constituted that she never had a mind or a wish of her own, but preferred to sympathize always with the minds and wishes of others. Above all – I need not say it – she was pure.

The Death of the Moth: Professions for Women

This I believe to be a very common experience with women writers – they are impeded by the extreme conventionality of the other sex.

The Death of the Moth: Professions for Women

It would be a thousand pities if women wrote like men, or lived like men or looked like men, for if two sexes are quite inadequate, considering the vastness and variety of the world, how should we manage with one only?

A Room of One's Own, V

… I went on amateurishly to sketch a plan of the soul so that in each of us two powers preside, one male, one female; and in the man's brain the man predominates over the woman, and in the woman's brain the woman predominates over the man. The normal and comfortable state of being is that when the two live in harmony together, spiritually co-operating …. Coleridge perhaps meant this when he said that a great mind is androgynous.

A Room of One's Own, VI

It is fatal to be a man or a woman pure and simple; one must be woman-manly or man-womanly.

... Some collaboration has to take place in the mind between the woman and the man before the act of creation can be accomplished. Some marriage of opposites has to be consummated.

A Room of One's Own, VI

There is someting maniacal in masculine vanity.

Diary, 28 July 1922

Women have served all these centuries as looking-glasses possessing the magic and delicious power of reflecting the figure of man at twice its natural size.

A Room of One's Own, II

I had been drawing a face, a figure. It was the face and the figure of Professor von X. engaged in writing his monumental work entitled *The Mental, Moral, and Physical Inferiority of the Female Sex*.

... England is under the rule of a patriarchy. Nobody in their senses could fail to detect the dominance of the professor. His was the power and the money and the influence. He was the proprietor of the paper and its editor and sub-editor. He was the Foreign Secretary and the Judge. He was the cricketer; he owned the racehorses and the yachts. He was the director of the company that pays two hundred per cent to its shareholders.

... Possibly when the professor insisted a little too emphatically upon the inferiority of women, he was concerned not with their inferiority, but with his own superiority.

... Walk through the Admiralty Arch ... or any other avenue given up to trophies and cannon, and reflect upon the kind of glory celebrated there. Or watch in the spring sunshine the stockbroker and the great barrister going indoors to make money and more money and more money ....

A Room of One's Own, II

For here again we come within range of that very interesting and obscure masculine complex which has had so much influence upon the woman's movement; that deep-seated desire, not so much that she shall be inferior as that he shall be superior ....

The history of men's opposition to women's emancipation is more interesting perhaps than the story of that emancipation itself.

A Room of One's Own, III

... now I'm going to be paid back for telling him he'd write 'little books' .... The vanity of men was immeasurable.

The Years: Present Day

Then again although it is true that we women can write articles or send letters to the Press – the decision what to print, what not to print – is entirely in the hands of your sex.

Your class [men] has been educated at public schools and universities for five or six hundred years, ours for sixty.

Your clothes in the first place make us gape with astonishment. How many, how splendid, how extremely ornate they are – the clothes worn by the educated man in his public capacity! Now you dress in violet; a jewelled crucifix swings on your breast; now your shoulders are covered with lace; now furred with ermine; now slung with many linked chains set with precious stones. Now you wear wigs on your heads, rows of graduated curls descend to your necks ... the splendour of your public attire is dazzling.

Obviously the connection between dress and war is not far to seek; your finest clothes are those you wear as soldiers. Since the red and the gold, the brass and the feathers are discarded upon active service, it is plain that their expensive and not, one might suppose, hygienic splendour is invented partly in order to impress the beholder with the majesty of the military office, partly in order through their vanity to induce young men to become soldiers.

Three Guineas, I

Meanwhile, do cast your mind further that way: about sharing life after the war: about pooling men's and women's work: about the possibility, if disarmament comes, of removing men's disabilities. Can one change sex characteristics? How far is the women's movement a remarkable experiment in that transformation? Mustn't our next task be the emancipation of man? How can we alter the crest and the spur of the fighting cock?

Letter, 22 June 1940

People

Why is it that relations between different people were so unsatisfactory, so fragmentary, so hazardous and words so dangerous that the instinct to sympathise with another human being was an instinct to be examined carefully and probably crushed.

The Voyage Out, XIV

It is no use trying to sum people up. One must follow hints, not exactly what is said, nor yet entirely what is done ....

Jacob's Room, III

We start transparent, and then the cloud thickens. All history backs our pane of glass. To escape is vain.

Jacob's Room, IV

It seems that a profound, impartial, and absolutely just opinion of our fellow-creatures is utterly unknown.

Jacob's Room, V

The body is harnessed to a brain. Beauty goes hand in hand with stupidity.

Jacob's Room, VI

Every face, every shop, bedroom window, public-house, and dark square is a picture feverishly turned – in search of what? It is the same with books. What do we seek through millions of pages?

Jacob's Room, VIII

The truth is people scarcely care for each other. They have this insane instinct for life. But they never become attached to anything outside themselves.
                              A Writer's Diary, 4 June 1923

The compensation of growing old ... was simply this; that the passions remain as strong as ever, but one has gained – at last! – the power which adds the supreme flavour to existence – the power of taking hold of experience, of turning it round, slowly, in the light.

What can one know even of the people one lives with every day? are we not all prisoners?
                              Mrs Dalloway

I like people to be unhappy because I like them to have souls. We all have, doubtless, but I like the suffering soul which confesses itself. I distrust this hard, this shiny, this enamelled content.
                              Letter, 22 September 1926

Who knows what we are, what we feel? Who knows even at the moment of intimacy, This is knowledge?
                              To the Lighthouse: The Lighthouse

Nature who has played so many queer tricks upon us, making us so unequally of clay and diamonds, of rainbow and granite, and stuffed them into a case of the most incongruous ....
                              Orlando, II

There is much to support the view that it is clothes that wear us and not we them; we may make them take the mould of arm or breast, but they mould our hearts, our brains, our tongues to their liking.
                              Orlando, IV

We are not slaves bound to suffer incessantly
unrecorded petty blows on our bent backs. We are
not sheep either, following a master. We are
creators.

The Waves: 'How fair, how strange'

It is strange that we who are capable of so much
suffering, should inflict so much suffering.

The Waves: 'Now to sum up'

We do not know our own souls, let alone the souls
of others. Human beings do not go hand in hand
the whole stretch of the way. There is a virgin forest
in each; a snowfield where even the print of birds'
feet is unknown.

The Moment: On being, III

... if we dont know ourselves how can we know
other people ....

The Years: Present Day

We're all afraid of each other ... afraid of what? Of
criticism, of laughter; of people who think
differently ....   *The Years*: Present Day

Pleasure is increased by sharing it. Does the same
hold good of pain .... Is that the reason why we all
talk so much of ill-health – because sharing things
lessens things? Give pain, give pleasure an outer
body, and by increasing the surface diminish them.

The Years: Present Day

Before we part, ladies and gentlemen, before we go
.... Let's talk in words of one syllable, without
larding, stuffing or cant.... And calmly consider
ourselves. Some bony. Some fat .... Liars most of
us. Thieves too .... The poor are as bad as the rich
are. Perhaps worse. Don't hide among rags. Or let
our cloth protect us. Or for the matter of that book
learning; or skilful practice on pianos; or laying on
of paint. Or presume there's innocency in
childhood. Consider the sheep. Or faith in love.
Consider the dogs. Or virtue in those that have
grown white hairs. Consider the gun slayers, bomb
droppers here or there. They do openly what we do
slyly .... Then there's the amiable condescension of
the lady of the manor – the upper class manner.
And buying shares in the market to sell 'em ....
O we're all the same.

Between the Acts

From this I reach what I might call a philosophy; at
any rate it is a constant idea of mine, that behind
the cotton wool is hidden a pattern; that we – I
mean all human beings – are connected with this;
that the whole world is a work of art, that we are
parts of the work of art.

Moments of Being: A Sketch of the Past

'... I was going to drink to the human race. The
human race ... which is now in its infancy, may it
grow to maturity!'

The Years: Present Day

Life

... she held in her hands for one brief moment the globe which we spend our lives in trying to shape, round, whole, and entire from the confusion of chaos.
Night and Day, XXXIII

Why is life so tragic; so like a strip of pavement over an abyss.
Diary, 25 October 1920

Life's what you see in people's eyes; life's what they learn, and, having learnt it, never, though they seek to hide it, cease to be aware of – what? That life's like that, it seems.
Monday or Tuesday: An Unwritten Novel

In any case life is but a procession of shadows, and God knows why it is that we embrace them so eagerly, and see them depart with such anguish, being shadows.
Jacob's Room, V

The strange thing about life is that though the nature of it must have been apparent to every one for hundreds of years, no one has left any adequate account of it.
Jacob's Room, VIII

It is thus that we live, they say, driven by an unseizable force. They say that the novelists never catch it; that it goes hurtling through their nets and leaves them torn to ribbons. This, they say, is what we live by – this unseizable force.
Jacob's Room, XII

Then … there was the terror; the overwhelming
incapacity, one's parents giving it into one's hands,
this life, to be lived to the end, to be walked with
serenely; there was in the depths of her heart an
awful fear.

Mrs Dalloway

Look within and life, it seems, is very far from
being 'like this'. Examine for a moment an ordinary
mind on an ordinary day. The mind receives a
myriad impressions – trivial, fantastic, evanescent,
or engraved with the sharpness of steel. From all
sides they come, an incessant shower of
innumerable atoms; and as they fall, as they shape
themselves into the life of Monday or Tuesday, the
accent falls differently from of old; the moment of
importance came not here but there; …
    … Life is not a series of gig lamps symmetrically
arranged; life is a luminous halo, a semi-
transparent envelope surrounding us from the
beginning of consciousness to the end.

The Common Reader, First Series: Modern Fiction

And yet the only exciting life is the imaginary one.

A Writer's Diary, 21 April 1928

How little one counts, I think: how little any one
counts; how fast & furious & masterly life is; & how
all these thousands are swimming for dear life.

A Writer's Diary, 27 October 1928

Now is life very solid, or very shifting? I am
haunted by the two contradictions. This has gone
on for ever; will last for ever, goes down to the
bottom of the world – this moment I stand on. Also
it is transitory, flying, diaphanous. I shall pass like

a cloud on the waves. Perhaps it may be that
though we change; one flying after another, so
quick, so quick, yet we are somehow successive, &
continuous – we human beings; & show the light
through. But what is the light? I am impressed by
the transitoriness of human life ....

A Writer's Diary, 4 January 1929

... if I had time to prove it, the truth of one's
sensations is not in the fact, but in the reverberation.

Letter, 9 January 1929

... Why is human life made up of such incongruous
things, and why are all one's events so perfectly
irrational that a good biographer would be forced
to ignore them entirely?

Letter, 25 August 1929

For, Lord, Lord, how much one lacks – how
fumbling and inexpert one is, never yet to have
learnt the hang of life – to have peeled that
particular orange.

Letter, 4 October 1929

'Among the tortures and devastations of life is this
then – our friends are not able to finish their stories.'

The Waves: 'Now,' said Bernard, 'the time has come'

'Let us again pretend that life is a solid substance,
shaped like a globe, which we turn about in our
finger. Let us pretend that we can make out a plain
and logical story, so that when one matter is
despatched – love for instance – we go on, in an
orderly manner, to the next.'

The Waves: 'Now, to sum up' said Bernard

Now I believe courage to be the greatest of human virtues, and the only gift we can impart.
 … life is of a hardness that still fairly terrifies me.

Letter, 1 March 1937

When shall we be free? When shall we live adventurously, wholly, not like cripples in a cave?

The Years, 1937

… Millions of things came back to her. Atoms danced apart and massed themselves. But how did they compose what people called a life?
 'Pity one can't live again,' …
 There must be another life, here and now …. This is too short, too broken. We know nothing, even about ourselves. We're only just beginning … to understand, here and there.
 Does everything then come over again a little differently? … If so, is there a pattern; a theme, recurring like music; half remembered, half foreseen? … a gigantic pattern, momentarily perceptible? … But who makes it? Who thinks it?

The Years: Present Day

Yes, I was thinking: we live without a future. That's what's queer: with our noses pressed to a closed door.

A Writer's Diary, 26 January 1941

Illness & Doctors

Considering how common illness is ... it becomes strange indeed that illness has not taken its place with love and battle and jealousy among the prime themes of literature. Novels, one would have thought, would have been devoted to influenza; epic poems to typhoid; odes to pneumonia, lyrics to toothache. But no; ... literature does its best to maintain that its concern is with the mind; that the body is a sheet of plain glass through which the soul looks straight and clear, and, save for one or two passions such as desire and greed, is null, and negligible and non existent. On the contrary, the very opposite is true ....

... The creature within can only gaze through the pane – smudged or rosy; it cannot separate off from the body like the sheath of a knife or the 'pod' of a pea for a single instant; it must go through the whole unending procession of changes, heat and cold, comfort and discomfort, hunger and satisfaction, health and illness, until there comes the inevitable catastrophe; the body smashes itself to smithereens, and the soul (it is said) escapes. But of all this daily drama of the body there is no record.

... Those great wars which the body wages with the mind a slave to it, in the solitude of the bedroom against the assaults of fever or the oncome of melancholia are neglected.

... There is, let us confess it (and illness is the great confessional) a childish outspokenness in illness; things are said, truths blurted out, which the cautious respectability of health conceals.

The Moment: On being ill

I can't conceive how anybody can be fool enough to believe in a doctor. Letter, 26 November 1904

To his patients he [Sir William Bradshaw] gave three-quarters of an hour; and in this exacting science which has to do with what, after all, we know nothing about – the nervous system, the human brain – a doctor loses his sense of proportion, as a doctor he fails. Health we must have and health is proportion; ....
   ... Worshipping proportion, Sir William not only prospered himself but made England prosper, secluded her lunatics, forbade childbirth, penalized despair, made it impossible for the unfit to propagate their views until they, too, shared his sense of proportion – his if they were men, Lady Bradshaw's if they were women ....
Mrs Dalloway

What business had the Bradshaws to talk of death at her party? A young man had killed himself ....
   ... But this young man who had killed himself .... Suppose he ... had gone to Sir William Bradshaw, a great doctor, yet to her obscurely evil, without sex or lust, extremely polite to women, but capable of some indescribable outrage – forcing your soul, that was it – that if this young man had gone to him, and Sir William had impressed him, like that, with his power, might not he have then said (indeed she felt it now), Life is made intolerable; they make life intolerable, men like that?
Mrs Dalloway

'Doctors know very little about the body; absolutely nothing about the mind.'
The Years: Present Day

Food & Wine

Suppose one had wine every day, at every meal –
What an enchanted world!   Letter, 31 March 1928

The human frame being what it is, heart, body and
brain all mixed together, and not contained in
separate compartments as they will be no doubt in
another million years, a good dinner is of great
importance to good talk. One cannot think well,
love well, sleep well, if one has not dined well.
                                        A Room of One's Own, I

These delicious mouthfuls of roast duck, fitly piled
with vegetables, following each other in exquisite
rotation of warmth, weight, sweet and bitter, past
my palate, down my gullet, into my stomach, have
stabilized my body. I feel quiet, gravity, control. All
is solid now. Instinctively my palate now requires
and anticipates sweetness and lightness, something
sugared and evanescent; and cool wine, fitting
glove-like over those finer nerves that seem to
tremble from the roof of my mouth and make it
spread (as I drink) into a domed cavern, green with
vine leaves, musk-scented, purple with grapes.
                          The Waves: 'How fair, How strange'

So back to a first rate dinner – a dinner thought out,
& presided over by a graceful young chef …. Our
dinner was rich & thoughtful: I had mushrooms in
cream. And I observed the way a good waiter
serves a dish with infinite care & respect, as if
handling something precious.
                                        Diary, 29 May 1935

Heaven above us, what immortal geese must have gone to make it! It was fresh as a dockleaf, pink as mushrooms, pure as first love .... My word what a pie!

Letter, 26? December 1937

Oh the vintage at Cassis! Just what my eyes crack to see. The one thing in the world I was born to describe.

Letter, 8 October 1938

... how it liberates the soul to drink a bottle of good wine daily and sit in the sun ....

Letter, 18 June 1939

Words, Letters & Memoirs

When I cannot see words curling like rings of
smoke round me I am in darkness – I am nothing.

The Waves: 'How fair, How strange'

The words of authority are corrupted by those who
speak them.

The Waves: 'Now', said Bernard, 'the time has come'

Nothing should be named lest by so doing we
change it.

The Waves: 'The complexity of things …'

The words we seek hang close to the tree. We come
at dawn and find them sweet beneath the leaf.

Jacob's Room, VIII

Ah, but when the post knocks and the letter comes
always the miracle seems repeated – speech
attempted. Venerable are letters, infinitely brave,
forlorn, and lost.

Life would split asunder without them.

Jacob's Room, VIII

If the art of letter writing consists in exciting the
emotions, in bringing back the past, in reviving a
day, a moment, nay a very second, of past time,
then these obscure correspondents, with their hasty
haphazard ways, their gibes and flings, their
irreverence and mockery, their careful totting up of
days and dates, their general absorption in the
moment and entire carelessness what posterity will
think of them, beat Cowper, Walpole, and Edward

Fitzgerald hollow. Yes, but what to do with them?
The question remains, for as one reads it becomes
perfectly plain that the art of letter writing has now
reached a stage ... where it is not dead – that is the
last word to apply to it – but so much alive as to be
quite unprintable. The best letters of our time are
precisely those that can never be published.

The Captain's Death Bed: Modern Letters

They [the Brownings] have become two of the most
conspicuous figures in that bright and animated
company of authors who, thanks to our modern
habit of writing memoirs and printing letters and
sitting to be photographed, live in the flesh, not
merely as of old in the word; are known by their
hats, not merely by their poems ....

How far we are going to read a poet when we can
read about a poet is a problem to lay before
biographers.

The Common Reader, Second Series: 'Aurora Leigh'

Here I come to one of the memoir writer's
difficulties – one of the reasons why, though I read
so many, so many are failures. They leave out the
person to whom things happened. The reason is
that it is so difficult to describe any human being.

Moments of Being: A Sketch of the Past

Bloomsbury & the Intellect

Where they seem to me to triumph is in having worked out a view of life which was not by any means corrupt or sinister or merely intellectual; rather ascetic and austere indeed; ....

Letter, 1 May 1925

If Bloomsbury had produced only Roger [Fry], it could be on a par with Athens at its prime.

Letter, 27 December 1928

It is true I wrote books and some of those books, like the Common reader, A Room of one's Own and Three Guineas ... have sold many thousand copies. That is, I did my best to make them reach a wider circle than a little private circle of exquisite and cultivated people. And to some extent I succeeded. Leonard too is Bloomsbury. He has spent half his life in writing books like International Government, like The Barbarians at the gate ...; and to create a League of Nations. Maynard Keynes is Bloomsbury .... These are facts about Bloomsbury and they do seem to me to prove that they have done their very best to make humanity in the mass appreciate what they knew and saw.

Letter, 24 August 1940

Now there can be no two opinions as to what a highbrow is. He is the man or woman of thoroughbred intelligence who rides his mind at a gallop across country in pursuit of an idea. That is why I have always been so proud to be called highbrow.

By a lowbrow is meant of course a man or a woman of thoroughbred vitality who rides his body in pursuit of a living at a gallop across life. That is why I honour and respect lowbrows – and I have never known a highbrow who did not.

The middlebrow is the man, or woman, of middlebred intelligence who ambles and saunters now on this side of the hedge, now on that, in pursuit of no single object, neither art itself nor life itself, but both mixed indistinguishably, and rather nastily, with money, fame, power, or prestige. The middlebrow curries favour with both sides equally.

The Death of the Moth: Middlebrow

Other Writers

I should be reading *Ulysses* and fabricating my case for and against .... An illiterate, underbred book it seems to me; the book of a self taught working man, and we all know how distressing they are, how egoistic, insistent, raw, striking and ultimately nauseating.

A Writer's Diary, 16 August 1922

I dislike Ulysses more and more – that is I think it more and more unimportant & dont even trouble conscientiously to make out its meanings.

Diary, 26 August 1922

I finished Ulysses and think it a mis-fire. Genius it has, I think; but of the inferior water. The book is diffuse. It is brackish. It is pretentious. It is underbred, not only in the obvious sense, but in the literary sense.

A Writer's Diary, 6 September 1922

Ulysses was a memorable catastrophe – immense in daring, terrific in disaster.

The Common Reader, First Series: How it strikes a contemporary

Then Joyce is dead; Joyce about a fortnight younger than I am. I remember Miss Weaver, in wool gloves, bringing Ulysses in typescript to our tea table at Hogarth House ... I bought the blue paper book and read it here one summer I think with spasms of wonder, of discovery, and then again, with long lapses of intense boredom.

A Writer's Diary, 15 January 1941

I am also reading D.H.L. [D.H. Lawrence] with the usual sense of frustration: and that he and I have too much in common – the same pressure to be ourselves: so that I don't escape when I read him: am suspended: what I want is to be made free of another world ....

But it's the preaching that rasps me.... He died though at 45. And why does Aldous say he was an 'artist'? Art is being rid of all preaching: things in themselves; the sentence in itself beautiful: multitudinous seas; daffodils that come before the swallow dares: whereas Lawrence would only say what proved something.

A Writer's Diary, 2 October 1932

One of the curious qualities of *Sons and Lovers* is that one feels an unrest, a little quiver and shimmer in his page, as if it were composed of separate gleaming objects, by no means content to stand still and be looked at ....

The only thing that we are given to rest upon, to expand upon, to feel to the limits of our powers is some rapture of physical being .... The book therefore excites, irritates, moves, changes, seems full of stir and unrest and desire for something withheld, like the body of the hero .... For the fact that he, Lawrence, like Paul, was a miner's son, and that he disliked his conditions, gave him a different approach to writing from those who have a settled station and enjoy circumstances which allow them to forget what those circumstances are.

The Moment

Disappointed, reading lightly though, by *The man who died*, D.H.L.'s last. Reading *Sons and Lovers* first then the last I seem to span the measure of his powers & trace his decline. A kind of Guy Fawkes dressing up grew on him it seems, in spite of the lovely silver-bright writing here and there: something sham. Making himself into a God, I suppose.

Diary, 28 May 1931

Indeed I don't see how much faith in her [Katherine Mansfield] as woman or writer can survive that sort of story. I shall have to accept the fact, I'm afraid, that her mind is a very thin soil, laid an inch or two deep upon very barren rock. For Bliss is long enough to give her a chance of going deeper. Instead she is content with superficial smartness; and the whole conception is poor, cheap, not the vision, however imperfect, of an interesting mind. She writes badly too.

A Writer's Diary, 7 August 1918

Katherine [Mansfield] has been dead a week.... At that one feels – What? A shock of relief? – a rival the less? Then confusion at feeling so little – then, gradually, blankness & disappointment. ... More generously I felt, But though I can do this better than she could, where is she, who could do what I can't.

Then, as usual with me, visual impressions kept coming & coming before me – always of Katherine putting on a white wreath, & leaving us, called away; made dignified, chosen. And then one pitied her. And one felt her reluctant to wear that wreath, which was an ice cold one. And she was only 33 .... And I was jealous of her writing – the only writing I have ever been jealous of.

Diary, 16 January 1923

Coda

No: I intend no introspection. I mark Henry James'
sentence: observe perpetually. Observe the oncome
of age. Observe greed. Observe my own
despondency. By that means it becomes
serviceable. Or so I hope. I insist upon spending my
time to the best advantage. I will go down with my
colours flying.

A Writer's Diary, 8 March 1941

In short, every secret of a writer's soul, every
experience of his life, every quality of his mind is
written large in his works, yet we require critics to
explain the one and biographers to expound the
other. That time hangs heavy on people's hands is
the only explanation of the monstrous growth.

Orlando, IV